Mysterious Encounters

The Loch Ness Monster

by Peggy J. Parks

KIDHAVEN PRESS

An imprint of Thomson Gale, a part of The Thomson Corporation

THOMSON

™

GALE

Detroit • New York • San Francisco • San Diego • New Haven, Conn. • Waterville, Maine • London • Munich

For more information, contact
KidHaven Press
27500 Drake Rd.
Farmington Hills, MI 48331-3535
Or you can visit our Internet site at http://www.gale.com

LIBRARY OF CONGRESS CATALOGING-IN-PUBLICATION DATA

Parks, Peggy J., 1951–
   The Loch Ness Monster / by Peggy J. Parks.
     p. cm. — (Mysterious encounters)
   Includes bibliographical references and index.
   ISBN 0-7377-3519-8 (hard cover : alk. paper) 1. Loch Ness monster—Juvenile literature. I. Title. II. Series.
   QL89.2.L6P38 2006
   001.944—dc22
                           2006007126

Contents

Chapter 1

THE GREAT BEAST OF THE LOCH

I n 1979, a researcher named Alastair Boyd experienced something he will never forget. He was on the shores of Loch Ness, an enormous lake in Scotland. Suddenly he spotted a creature in the water that was unlike anything he had ever seen before. He was positive that it was the Loch Ness Monster, which is often called Nessie. Afterward, Boyd stated, "I know that the thing I saw was not a log or an otter or a wave, or anything like that. . . . It came heaving out of the water, something like a whale. . . . It was totally **extraordinary** . . . the most amazing thing I've ever seen in my life."[1]

Over the years, hundreds of people have reported sightings like Boyd's. Although no two people have

The great beast known as the Loch Ness Monster may look something like this illustration.

described the beast exactly the same, their stories have many things in common. For instance, most observers said the creature was dark in color, perhaps gray or brownish-black. They said its skin looked rough, but did not appear to have scales like a fish. The beast was said to be huge, about 30 feet (9.1m) long, or possibly even longer. More than half of the observers said it had a long, skinny neck and small head similar to a dinosaur's. Many noticed two to three large humps on its back, and some said it had flippers. When people saw the creature in the water,

Nessie is said to lurk in the deep, dark waters of Loch Ness, seen here from the air.

it was often romping and splashing, but sometimes it was quite still. Whenever it heard a noise, they said, it quickly swam away.

A Place of Mystery

The **loch** (Scottish Gaelic for "lake") where the beast is said to live is a mysterious place. It was created thousands of years ago, during a period known as the Ice Age. At that time, Scotland was covered with **glaciers** that were thousands of feet high. When the Ice Age ended and the glaciers retreated, a huge, gaping hole had been gouged in the earth. Over the years, it came to be known as Loch Ness. It is an immense body of fresh water that is bigger than all the other lakes in Great Britain put together.

The water in the loch is very deep and cold. It is also black as soot—so black that no one can see more than a foot or two below the surface. In 1932, three professional divers found this out for themselves. They were sent into the loch to recover the body of an accident victim who was feared drowned. After going about 150 feet (46m) down, the divers returned to the surface scared and shaken. They reported that while they were underwater, they could see absolutely nothing in the eerie darkness.

For the people who believe in Nessie, it makes sense that such a creature would live in the loch. After all, the deep, dark water would provide the perfect hiding place. Some scientists believe there may even

Loch Ness, Scotland

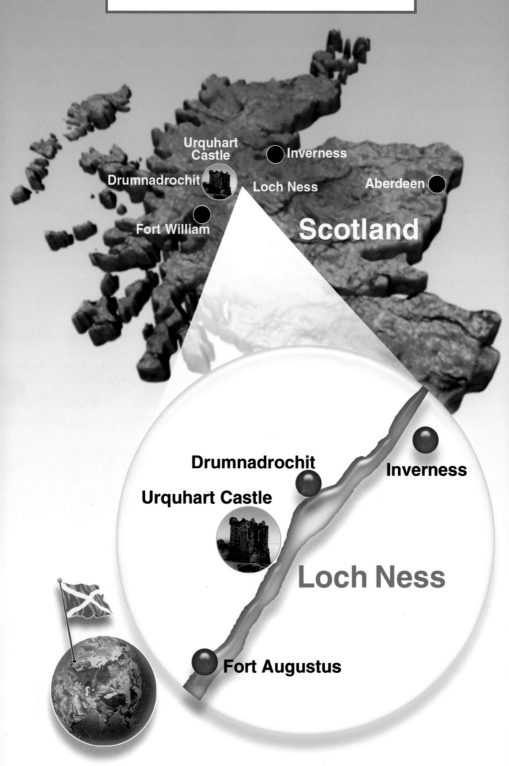

be huge underwater caves in the loch. Still others speculate that there might be hidden tunnels that connect the loch to the sea. No one knows if these things are true or not. However, the idea that they could exist fuels the belief that Nessie is alive and real.

A Fearsome Creature

The people who claim to have seen the Loch Ness Monster often describe it as scary looking, but not especially fierce or threatening. However, that was not the case with the first known sighting. In a biography of an Irish monk named Saint Columba, Saint Adamnan wrote about the monk's triumph over a fearsome water beast. The encounter supposedly happened in the year A.D. 565, when Saint Columba arrived on the banks of Loch Ness. He ordered one of his men to swim across the water and retrieve a small boat that was moored on the other side. An enormous beast noticed the commotion the man was making as he swam. It rose up and began roaring loudly as it rushed toward the man with its mouth open. Saint Columba realized that the man was about to be attacked and killed, so he raised his hand and made the sign of the cross in the air. Then in a loud, booming voice, he ordered the ferocious beast, in the name of God, to leave the man alone. Saint Adamnan wrote that the beast obeyed, and "at the voice of the saint the monster was terrified and fled more quickly than if it had been pulled back with ropes."[2]

In this illustration, Saint Columba commands the monster of Loch Ness to be still.

Sightings Start to Soar

Over the centuries that followed, stories of the water beast were common among those who lived around Loch Ness. Some people were convinced that they had a monster for a neighbor. One of the believers was Ian Milne, who lived in a village near the loch. He told about a warm summer day in 1930 when he was fishing with some friends. Suddenly they noticed something thrashing in the water, throwing spray high into the air. Then they saw what was causing it—a strange beast that Milne believed was about 20 feet (6.1m) long. He later stated that it was "without doubt a living creature . . . certainly not a basking shark or seal or a school of otters or anything normal."[3]

Before the 1930s, accounts such as Milne's were rare. When people did report sightings of a beast in Loch Ness, the news was mostly confined to the local area. The rest of the world was not really aware that such a monster might exist—but that all changed in 1933. Huge areas of forest were cleared to build a new road along the northern shoreline of the loch. When it was completed, the view of the water was

Exaggerated Story?

According to Saint Adamnan, Saint Columba was the first to encounter the enormous Loch Ness creature in A.D. 565. British professor Charles Thomas translated and studied Adamnan's original Latin text. He concluded that the "beast" was probably a large water mammal, such as a walrus or seal.

clearer than ever before. As a result, more and more people started reporting encounters with the beast.

In the six months after the new road was built, there were at least thirty reported sightings. Newspapers such as the *Scotsman* and the *Inverness Courier* ran long, detailed articles about them. Radio stations interrupted their regular programs to report the latest monster-related information. Soon the news spread to other parts of the world. Reporters from all over traveled to Loch Ness to get details about the mysterious water beast.

Nessie makes an appearance in this famous 1934 photo, later proven to be a hoax.

One Scientist's Theory

Loch Ness is known for its large, sloshing waves. These are sometimes produced by seismic activity, the same shock waves within Earth that can cause earthquakes. Italian geologist Luigi Piccardi believes the commotions people have seen, as well as the noises they have heard, were caused by seismic activity, rather than any sort of swimming beast.

Are They Making It Up?

One of the most famous reported encounters with Nessie involved a British surgeon named R. Kenneth Wilson. He claimed that in April 1934, he saw the enormous beast as he was driving along the shore of the loch. He even gave a picture of the creature to a London newspaper called the *Daily Mail*. The paper published an article about Wilson, along with the photograph. Because the doctor was highly respected, few people doubted his story. However, sixty years after the photo was released, it was proven to be a fake. Instead of a real beast, the photograph actually showed a toy monster floating on a miniature submarine.

Dozens of other encounters have also been proven to be **hoaxes**. But there have also been sightings that were believable, as well as unexplainable—and many involved respectable people. Police officers have reported seeing the beast, as have lawyers, priests, schoolteachers, businesspeople, and scientists. These people knew their stories would be considered far-fetched by nonbelievers. Still, they have no doubt that they saw Nessie, as retired police detective Ian Cameron explains: "In no way am I even attempting to convert anybody to the religion of the object in Loch Ness. . . . But I saw it, and nothing can take that away."[4]

Chapter 2

A SWIMMING MONSTER

I t was June 1965 when Ian Cameron spotted the Loch Ness Monster. As he was fishing in the loch, a large object came up out of the water and then disappeared. He had no idea what the thing was, so he continued fishing and waited for it to reappear. Then he saw it again—and this time it was zooming toward him through the water. He was positive it was some sort of strange water beast that he thought resembled a large black whale. Cameron says that if he had not seen it with his own eyes, he would likely not have believed it.

Enormous Creature, Monstrous Waves

Like Cameron, most people who claim to have seen the Loch Ness Monster saw it in the water. Some say it was leisurely floating or swimming. At other times, the beast was seen racing across the loch as fast as a powerful motorboat.

Mr. and Mrs. John Mackay reported a sighting in April 1933. The Mackays, who managed a hotel called the Drumnadro-chit, were taking a drive along the loch. The water was as smooth as glass,

Ian Cameron (right) was fishing near Urquhart Castle (below) when he saw the strange beast of Loch Ness.

without even a ripple. Suddenly Mrs. Mackay noticed a commotion on the water and cried out to her husband to stop. He slammed on the brakes, and the two of them stared in disbelief at a huge whale-like animal.

Later, the Mackays told the story to Alex Campbell, a reporter for the *Inverness Courier.* Campbell wrote in his article that the creature had been "rolling and plunging for fully a minute . . . and the water cascading and churning like a simmering cauldron. Soon, however, it disappeared in a boiling mass of foam."[5] The article stated that the Mackays knew this was no fish or ordinary loch creature. It was just too enormous. They said the beast was so big that when it took its final plunge under the water, it created waves big enough to have been caused by a ship.

A Thrilling Experience

Three years after the Mackays' sighting, Marjory Moir had her own encounter with the water beast. Moir lived near the loch in the town of Inverness. She said she was taking a drive with her family on an October afternoon. All of a sudden her sister shouted that she had seen the monster. Everyone got out of the car and ran down to the shore. Later, Moir wrote about her experience in a letter to a friend: "There, before us . . . was this wonderful creature. It was a perfect view, if we had a camera the most convincing picture of the Monster ever taken could have been obtained, but alas! we had neither camera nor binoculars."[6] Moir further described the beast as dark gray, about 30 feet (9.1m) long, with three distinct humps on its back. As she and her family continued to watch it, they saw that it was mostly quiet. It often dipped its head into the water, because it was either drinking or playing. Moir wrote that they watched in awe and amazement for about five to eight minutes. Then the creature abruptly turned away from the shoreline and shot across the loch at great speed. Moir said it was both

powerful and graceful, and that being able to see it was thrilling.

From Skeptic to Believer

Dorothy Fraser was also amazed at how fast the monster swam through the water. At the time she reportedly saw it, she lived in a cottage overlooking Loch Ness. On a warm spring day in 1967 she was working in her garden. Much to her surprise, she noticed what she described as a big, gray-black oval mass come out of the loch. At first Fraser thought it

Those who have seen Nessie give remarkably similar descriptions of an enormous, prehistoric-looking sea creature.

might be a submarine, and she grabbed her binoculars to have a closer look. Then she realized it was an enormous water creature. She was so shocked that her knees got weak and the binoculars slipped out of her hands. She had never believed the stories about the monster. In fact, she often told other people that there was no such thing. Once she saw it for herself, however, she believed she had been wrong.

Fraser's cottage was perched high on a hillside, so she had an excellent view of the water. She continued watching the creature as it swam. It moved out to the center of the loch and began gathering speed, until it was swimming faster and faster. Then in an instant it sank and was gone. Fraser describes the effect this had on the water: "All that was left was a wake, and you could have said it was from a **paddlesteamer**, the waves were so big."[7] After years of denying that a monster lived in Loch Ness, Fraser was now a firm believer.

"Oh, There's Nessie"

Unlike Fraser, Val Moffett had always believed in the Loch Ness Monster. Yet after living on the shores of the loch for a year, she had not seen it. Then one bright, sunny day in September 1990, she got her chance. According to Moffett, she was driving home from Inverness and glanced out toward the water. There she saw a large lump that she thought resembled a boat turned upside down. It looked to be about 30 feet (9.1m) long and 10 feet (3m) high, with skin that was a "sludgy" mixture of browns and greens. Trying to keep her eyes on the road, Moffett watched the creature on and off for a few seconds. She saw it three or four times before it disappeared. At that point, she thought to herself, "Oh, there's Nessie. 'Bout time I saw it. . . . And then something in the back of my head sort of said . . . 'That's got to be *the* Loch Ness Monster . . . and you're looking at the darn thing.'"[8] Moffett was so stunned at what she had just seen, she nearly drove her car off the road.

"I've Actually Seen It!"

Inverness resident Gary Campbell was also stunned when he saw Nessie in March 1996. Campbell, who worked as an accountant, was sitting by the loch doing paperwork. Suddenly, something in the water

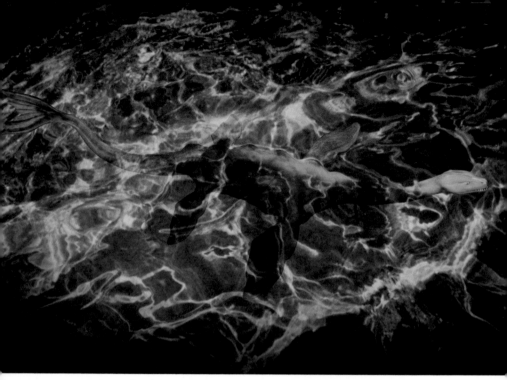

Nessie's dark coloring in this picture blends in easily with the black waters of Loch Ness.

caught his attention. Out of the corner of his eye, he noticed a large black hump come out of the water. When he turned to watch it, it disappeared, surfaced again, and then went back down. Campbell was positive it was not a seal or fish, or any sort of ordinary water creature. He said there was no doubt that it was the Loch Ness Monster. Later, he explained his reaction at the time of his encounter: "I thought . . . I've seen it! Good grief, after all these years being here and then thinking 'Heavens above!' you know, 'I've actually seen it!'"[9]

Chapter 3

"IT'S STILL SO VERY VIVID IN MY MIND"

Gary Campbell's sighting of the Loch Ness Monster was typical of most accounts because the beast was seen in the water. To this day, Nessie fans often keep a close watch on the loch because that is where they expect the creature to be. There are some eyewitnesses, however, who have encountered it in a very different way. They swear that they saw the monster on land.

"It Was Horrible"

One of the most famous of these land sightings was reported in July 1933. Mr. and Mrs. F.T.G. Spicer were driving home from the northern part of Scotland. To their amazement, a gigantic creature with a long, arched neck was emerging from the bushes. As soon as its enormous body was in plain sight, it shot across the road right in front of them. The Spicers

More than one beast may live in the depths of Loch Ness.

Monster Mania

In 1933, the same year the new road was completed along the shore of Loch Ness, a movie called *King Kong* opened in the United States. Before long, "monster fever" began spreading throughout the Western world. Some people say this explains the increased Nessie sightings during the same time period. They were likely caused by overactive imaginations stimulated by the popular monster movie.

Archaeologists sift through items found at Loch Ness during construction of the new road in 1933.

Nessie glides past Urquhart Castle in this illustration. While the monster's existence has not been proven, many people believe it is real.

described it as dark gray, much like an elephant, and said it was about 25 to 30 feet (7.6 to 9.1m) long. Although they had never seen anything like it before, they said the creature reminded them of an enormous snail.

The Spicers left the area where they had seen the beast. Along the way, they met William McCulloch, a man from a nearby village. When they told him what they had seen, he was astonished because a friend had reported seeing a similar creature. He rode his bicycle to the spot where the Spicers had their frightening encounter. There he observed that all plants and shrubs in the area had been totally crushed. He later said it looked as if a steamroller had run through and flattened everything in its path.

Mr. Spicer wrote to the *Inverness Courier,* and his letter appeared in the paper. He described the fear and disgust he and his wife had felt when they saw the beast: "It was horrible . . . . Whatever it is and it may be a land and water animal, I think it should be destroyed." [10] After the letter was published, news of the creature began to spread rapidly. Reporters began hounding the Spicers. Articles appeared in a number of newspapers and the couple became quite well known. The attention they received, however, was not positive. People often ridiculed them, accusing them of making the story up. Still, they stood by what they said and insisted they had seen the beast. They even offered to take a public oath to swear they were being honest. A few months later, a highly respected public official named Rupert Gould visited the Spicers. After talking with them, he was convinced they were telling the truth.

A Near Collision

Six months after the Spicers' sighting, the beast was spotted on land again—and this time it was almost struck by a motorcycle. Arthur Grant, a young veterinary student, was returning home from Inverness about 1:00 A.M. It was very dark, but the moon shone brightly in the sky. As Grant was just about to make a sharp turn, he noticed a large, dark creature near the bushes. Apparently frightened by the sound of the motorcycle, the beast lurched into the road

Pranksters Galore

Even when claims of encounters have seemed believable, they were undermined by deliberate hoaxes. For instance, soon after Arthur Grant reported seeing the beast on land, three-toed footprints and a pile of bones were found near the site where he saw it. According to author and science professor Henry H. Bauer, someone probably thought Grant's report was a good opportunity to play a joke or create a hoax by planting fake evidence.

Once claims of Nessie sightings became known, faked photos like this one flourished.

and crashed through the brush on the other side. Then it raced down to the loch and plopped into the water with an enormous splash. Grant jumped off his motorcycle and followed it. By the time he reached the shoreline, however, it had disappeared. The only signs that it had been there were ripples on the surface of the water.

Grant inspected the path the beast had taken. He marked the spot where he had seen it, and then went home and drew a sketch of the creature. He estimated that it was about 15 to 20 feet (4.6 to 6.1m) in length, and had a long neck, small head, and large oval eyes. Attached to its enormous body was a long tail like a kangaroo's that was rounded at the end. Grant recalled that the creature had two sets of flippers, which it used to propel itself across the road at a high rate of speed. Later, he was quoted as saying, "Knowing something of natural history, I can say that I have never seen anything in my life like the animal I saw."[11]

"He Said I Must Have Been Dreaming"

Alfred Cruickshank also claimed that he saw the strange beast while driving. His sighting occurred about ten years before Grant's. At that time, the new road along the loch had not yet been completed. Cruickshank, who was a chauffeur, was driving a Model T Ford along the bumpy, winding road. He drove up a hill and his headlights suddenly picked up a huge moving object. He said it had a large, humped body, a belly that trailed on the ground, and a long, thick tail. It moved slowly, as if it were waddling along on two legs. Cruickshank said the creature looked to be a dark olive color, but he could not tell for sure in the dim light. Unlike most other eyewitnesses, he did not remember the beast having much of a neck.

Shaken by what he had seen, he kept on driving. When he met up with his employer, the man noticed that his chauffeur was very pale. He asked Cruickshank what was wrong. "I told him what had happened, and he said I must have been dreaming,"[12] Cruickshank later stated. When he told others of his encounter, they did not believe him either. So he decided to keep quiet about it.

Monster on the Beach

Margaret Cameron also reportedly saw the beast on land, and she, too, kept quiet. She told only her parents and grandfather, who said they did not want anyone else to know. Cameron's sighting occurred during the early 1900s, when she was a young girl. She was with her brothers and sister playing on the beach. As they skipped stones across the water, they heard crackling noises coming from the trees. The sound got louder and louder, and the children knew that whatever was making the noises was getting closer. They stood there, terrified—and then an enor-

Living giant Am
compared with an
(Drawn to Scale

R. Brightwell.

Ten Feet.

fish and crayfish, and though able
ve quickly on occasion could
y put up the motor-launch speed
to the "monster," far be
th a sheep,
bians

A newspaper article from the 1930s shows a drawing of the enormous monster of Loch Ness.

mous creature with shiny gray skin came out of the trees. Because it was facing them head on they could not tell if it had a long or short neck, but they could see its huge body. As the beast lumbered along the beach toward the loch, the children could see two short, round feet at the front of its body. They watched it go into the water, and then the scared children ran away.

Many years later, Cameron described the frightening experience to BBC correspondent Nicholas Witchell: "When we got home we were all sick and couldn't take our tea. . . . It's still so very vivid in my mind—I'll never forget it." [13]

Chapter 4

NESSIE HUNTERS

L ike Margaret Cameron, most people who claim to have seen the Loch Ness Monster were caught off-guard when it appeared. Even if they had lived in Scotland their whole lives, their encounters were completely unexpected. There have been others, however, who were so determined to find the beast that they deliberately went hunting for it.

The most famous of these monster hunters was Tim Dinsdale, an **aeronautical engineer** from England. His curiosity about the beast began in 1959, when he read about it in a magazine article. Of particular interest was the mention of a Scottish doctor named Constance Whyte who had written a book called *More Than a Legend*. The book included photographs, sketches, and personal accounts from people who had seen the creature. Dinsdale was fascinated, as he later wrote: "I was mentally disturbed; jolted out of the rut of normal thinking by this detailed and strange account of the Monster." [14]

Thrashing its huge tail, the Loch Ness Monster swims near the loch's bottom in this illustration.

Captured on Film!

Dinsdale started researching the reported sightings, comparing and analyzing the descriptions of the beast. Then, in April 1960, he traveled to the Scottish Highlands. He planned to spend a week there in the hope of seeing Nessie for himself.

During his visit, Dinsdale kept a close watch on the loch. By the fifth day he was starting to get discouraged—but then his patience finally paid off. He had set up his movie camera on a hilltop overlooking the loch. Just as daylight began to fade, he saw what he described as "a violent disturbance—a churning ring of rough water, centring about what appeared to be two long black shadows, or shapes, rising and falling in the water!"[15] Convinced it was the monster, Dinsdale managed to catch the action on film. He jumped in his car and drove down to the shoreline. But by the time he got there, the water was still and there were no signs of any creature.

On the last day of his trip, Dinsdale decided to try one last time. He set up his camera inside the car and slowly drove down the hill toward the loch, filming all the way. When he was about halfway down, he spotted an object on the surface of the water. He stopped the car and grabbed his binoculars. It was the creature! He saw that it was reddish-brown and had a huge hump on its back. Dinsdale grabbed his movie camera and began

Nessie hunter Tim Dinsdale spent years trying to capture a clear image of the monster on film.

filming the beast as it swam. He later wrote: "I watched successive rhythmic bursts of foam break the surface—*paddle strokes:* with such a regular beat I instinctively began to count—one, two, three, four—pure white blobs of froth contrasting starkly against the black water."[16]

From Engineer to Monster Hunter

Dinsdale returned to England and turned the film over to British officials who specialized in analyzing photography. After a careful examination, they confirmed that the film was genuine. They also confirmed that there was something alive in the water, and that whatever sort of creature it was, it was quite large. Later, the film appeared on British television and generated a great deal of excitement about Nessie. Soon people were contacting Dinsdale to tell their own stories of encounters.

In July 1960, Dinsdale went back to Loch Ness and spent nine days there. Even though he did not see the beast, that did not discourage him. He had become totally captivated by it—so much so that he gave up his engineering career. He wanted to devote the rest of his life to pursuing the creature he had captured on film.

In the years that followed, Dinsdale visited the loch 56 times. Some of his trips lasted for weeks, and others lasted for months. His goal was to see the Loch Ness Monster again and get even better film. Nicholas Witchell describes Dinsdale's fierce devotion to hunting for the creature: "He spent many hundreds of days and nights afloat in the loch in his tiny motor cruiser *Water Horse*. It was a gruelling, frequently dreadfully uncomfortable and downright dangerous mission, facing the loch's many moods at

When Eyes Play Tricks

Many scientists insist that the moving objects people have seen when they explored the loch are nothing more than shadows. Other theories have included boat wakes, floating logs, large otters or seals—and especially sightseers with overactive imaginations.

Ripples trail a ferryboat on Loch Ness. Some Nessie sightings might be no more mysterious than boat wakes.

all hours and in all weather in such a small craft." [17] Dinsdale spotted the beast two more times, once in 1970 and again in 1971. To his great disappointment, he was not able to capture any significant footage. Yet he never gave up. He remained committed to hunting Nessie until his death in 1987.

Monster Detectives

During Dinsdale's early years pursing the creature, a group of Nessie enthusiasts formed the Loch Ness Phenomena Investigation Bureau. Their mission was to find evidence to prove that the monster was real.

Bureau members began their work in October 1962. They lived in trailers along the shoreline of the loch, and they took turns keeping watch. At night they were aided by huge searchlights that swept over the water. They had still cameras and movie cameras ready so if anyone noticed a disturbance, the group could immediately capture it on film. The bureau worked on the project for ten years. In that time there were several sightings, but none were considered very significant.

In 1972, the bureau teamed up with Boston's Academy of Applied Science, and together they planned several expeditions. Their boats were fitted with **sonar** equipment that used sound waves to sweep the loch. If the waves encountered a large object of any kind, echoes would bounce back to the **transponder**, or sending device. By counting the number of echoes, the size of the object could be de-

Although Tim Dinsdale never got a clear photo of Nessie, he worked tirelessly on the project until his death.

termined. The boats were also equipped with cameras that snapped pictures underwater.

An expedition in August 1972 was particularly eventful. Crew members were scouring the loch late at night when their sonar equipment suddenly recorded a large moving object. Peter Davies, a bureau member and the skipper of one of the boats, spoke to Witchell about the experience: "The wind dropped and the water settled down to become jelly calm. . . . Then it started—a big, black trace started to appear . . . it got bigger and blacker and thicker; we could hardly believe our eyes—something huge was moving down there, very near to where the camera was."[18] Adding to the intrigue were photographs that showed large flipper-like objects.

After the expedition ended, scientists examined the photos and sonar readings. They could not make a definite conclusion about whether or not the Loch Ness Monster existed. But they did confirm the possibility that a large, unknown aquatic beast could be living in the loch.

As technology becomes more sophisticated, perhaps one day the mystery of the Loch Ness Monster will be solved.

A Never-Ending Saga

The possibility that the creature might exist is precisely what keeps people all over the world fascinated with Nessie even today. Whether it was seen thrashing in the water or lumbering across the road, hundreds of observers swear they saw it. In the foreword to Witchell's book *The Loch Ness Story*, British scientist Sir Peter Scott said the saga of the monster is one that never ends. "Only by draining the loch could it ever be proved that no such animal exists," he wrote. "Although no specimen has so far been available for examination, it is still possible to keep an open mind." [19] Scott's words back up all the people who believe in Nessie. To them, there is no question that the mysterious beast lives in the loch. For true believers, the Loch Ness Monster is indeed alive and well—and no amount of scorn and ridicule will ever change their minds.

Notes

Chapter 1: The Great Beast of the Loch

1. Quoted in NOVA Online, "The Beast of Loch Ness," January 12, 1999. www.pbs.org/wgbh/nova/lochness/legend3.html.
2. Quoted in Nicholas Witchell, *The Loch Ness Story*. Lavenham, UK: Terence Dalton, 1974, p. 18.
3. Quoted in Witchell, *The Loch Ness Story*, p. 37.
4. Quoted in NOVA Online, "The Beast of Loch Ness," www.pbs.org/wgbh/nova/lochness/eyewitness.html.

Chapter 2: A Swimming Monster

5. Quoted in Dick Raynor, "A Brief Overview of 'Nessie' History," Loch Ness Investigation. www.lochnessinvestigation.org/history.html.
6. Quoted in Tim Dinsdale, *Loch Ness Monster*. London/Boston: Routledge & Kegan Paul, 1976, p. 93.
7. Quoted in Witchell, *The Loch Ness Story*, pp. 88–89.
8. Quoted in NOVA Online, "The Beast of Loch Ness," www.pbs.org/wgbh/nova/lochness/eyewitness.html.

9. Quoted in NOVA Online, "The Beast of Loch Ness," www.pbs.org/wgbh/nova/lochness/eyewitness.html.

Chapter 3: "It's Still So Very Vivid in My Mind"

10. Quoted in Witchell, *The Loch Ness Story,* pp. 118–19.
11. Quoted in Dinsdale, *Loch Ness Monster,* p. 35.
12. Quoted in Witchell, *The Loch Ness Story,* p. 117.
13. Quoted in Witchell, *The Loch Ness Story,* pp. 112–13.

Chapter 4: Nessie Hunters

14. Dinsdale, *Loch Ness Monster,* p. 3.
15. Dinsdale, *Loch Ness Monster,* p. 74.
16. Dinsdale, *Loch Ness Monster,* p. 79.
17. Witchell, *The Loch Ness Story,* p. 210.
18. Witchell, *The Loch Ness Story,* pp. 165–66.
19. Sir Peter Scott, foreword to Nicholas Witchell, *The Loch Ness Story,* p. vi.

Glossary

aeronautical engineer: A person who designs and constructs aircraft.

extraordinary: Remarkable; very unusual.

glaciers: Enormous masses of ice and snow.

hoaxes: Activities meant to trick or deceive.

loch: The Scottish Gaelic word for "lake."

paddle-steamer: A boat propelled by steam-powered paddle wheels.

sonar: Technology that measures the size of an object using sound waves.

transponder: The sending/receiving device of sonar equipment.

For Further Exploration

Books

Peggy J. Parks, *The Loch Ness Monster.* Detroit: Kid-Haven Press, 2005. Tells the story of the monster known as Nessie, who is said to live in Scotland's famous Loch Ness. Includes information about how people describe the beast, how often they have seen it, and the efforts to prove (and disprove) its existence throughout the years.

Holly Wallace, *The Mystery of the Loch Ness Monster.* Des Plaines, IL: Heinemann Library, 1999. Discusses how the Loch Ness Monster story began, eyewitness accounts, various efforts to discover and identify the creature, and possible explanations about what it could be.

Periodicals

Sharon J. Huntington, "Stalking Legendary Creatures," *Christian Science Monitor,* April 9, 2002.

Jamie Kiffel, "Could the Loch Ness Monster Exist? Decide for Yourself," *National Geographic Kids,* July/August 2004, pp. 38–39.

Web Sites

The Legend of Nessie (www.nessie.co.uk). People interested in the Loch Ness Monster will find a great deal of information on this site, including firsthand accounts of the beast, stories, scientific studies, and tales of hunting expeditions.

Nessie: The Loch Ness Monster Information Web Site (www.loch-ness.com). This site was created by Tony Harmsworth, who is considered an authority on Loch Ness and its many unexplained mysteries. It features underwater and surface photographs, eyewitness accounts, and information about many water creatures.

Nessie on the Net (www.lochness.com.uk). Nessie fans will likely find everything they need on this information-packed site. It features "Nessie News," records of sightings, photographs, facts and figures, and links to many other sites.

Index